THE SWISS COOKERY BOOK

KU-488-552

The Swiss Cookery Book

Recipes
from all cantons

Collected by
Helen Guggenbühl

Translated by
Mary Hottinger

Fifth printing

SCHWEIZER SPIEGEL VERLAG

By the same publishers

B. Bradfield

A POCKET HISTORY OF SWITZERLAND
with Historical Outline and Guide

Hans Huber

HOW SWITZERLAND IS GOVERNED

Walther Hofer

*NEUTRALITY AS THE PRINCIPLE
OF SWISS FOREIGN POLICY*

Adolf Guggenbühl

ZURICH PICTURE-BOX
36 coloured views and photographs of Zurich,
past and present

Copyright by Guggenbühl & Huber
Schweizer Spiegel Verlag Zürich 1953
Printed in Switzerland by City-Druck AG, Zürich
Illustrated by Werner Wälchli

CONTENTS

INTRODUCTION

The present booklet is intended to serve more than one purpose. Firstly, it is for use — it contains recipes which may be found interesting and useful especially at a time when meat is not plentiful. Secondly, it may help to guide the uninitiated in restaurants. Thirdly, it may be of use to the English and American housewife in Switzerland, confronted as she is with very different eating habits. And finally, it has a purpose which might be defined as local colour. Some of these recipes will hardly be tried out—certainly not the one beginning "Take 30 eggs"— but they are interesting in themselves as being old and original.

No visitor to Switzerland needs to be reminded of the excellence of Swiss cooking; the mere fact that so many chefs in big hotels are Swiss is a proof of it. But domestic cooking in Switzerland has a very marked character of its own which does not always come out in restaurants and hotels. It is, of course, as everywhere else the product of geography and history. Since Swiss democracy was built up from the bottom upward, we shall find eating habits taking something of the same course. There can be distinctly traced in them the influence of the first founders of the Confederation—the Alpine peasants and the smaller bourgeoisie of the towns.

Meat has no pride of place in Swiss cookery. It will be said, of course, that that is true of England and large sections of America. That is quite true, but it is taking a great effort of adaptation, to plan meatless meals in those countries, while plain meals without meat are a regular feature of the Swiss menu. For instance, a favourite evening dish is "Rösti", the Swiss version of sautéd potatoes, which is served with coffee and milk. The only disadvantage about rösti is that it takes quite a lot of butter. Then there are the "Wähen" (in French Switzerland, "tarte", though it is not so common in that part of the country as in Eastern Switzerland). This is a flat tart or flan made with pretty well anything you like—fruit, cheese, custard, bacon, even spinach. On Friday, which is a great cleaning day in Swiss households, the midday meal often consists of wähen of one or more kinds, served with coffee and milk. Even restaurants are now providing a "Wähenmenu" on Fridays.

As to vegetables, the English habit of serving plain boiled vegetables is not liked in Switzerland. It goes back, of course, to the time when English meat was the juiciest in the world. The collector of the recipes in this booklet has noted, however, that the habit of covering vegetables with other things—bacon, cheese, onions, sauces, or frying them in batter—is now rather old-fashioned, and that people are coming more and more to steam vegetables plainly in water and butter. There are, of course, a number of vegetables which are not known in England, though they figure in American cookery books—kohlrabi, for instance, or the succulent stalks of a very large kind of cabbage (Krautstiele), while fennel is quite a common dish. On the other hand, turnips do not seem to be obtainable in the Eastern part of Switzerland at any rate.

A great feature of Swiss cookery is fritters—almost anything can be dipped in batter and fried in olive oil or deep fat, or butter. Apple rings, bunches of cherries, sage leaves, hardboiled eggs, egg-plant, salsify, zucchini, fish, all these are used for fritters. Some are quite delicious, though it takes some heroism to make them.

Swiss confectionery too has a character of its own. There are the famous "Eieröhrli", incredibly thin brittle pancakes fried in butter in a pan too small for them, so that they crumple up; these belong to carnival time, and stand in heaps in confectioners' windows. Of "Krapfen", a kind of turnover filled with ground nuts and dried fruit, there are many varieties according to the locality. The recipes of two famous specialities have not been included here because they are never made at home—the famous pasty of Glarus, a covered tart made of layers of puff pastry and filled on one side with almond paste, on the other with jam; the second is the equally famous *Kirschtorte* of Zoug.

Cheese dishes, as might be expected, are rich and varied. From the different fondues of Geneva and Neuchatel to the cheese-dishes made by the Alpine dairymen, all are worth trying. Of course, part of the charm is the enormous variety of cheese available—one kind of fondue requires five different kinds of cheese, and many generations of experience must lie behind the exact mixture of cheeses in a number of recipes.

It will be noticed that there is only one fish recipe here, that for the famous salmon of Basle. It is given as a piece of local colour, since Basle has wonderful salmon, and in the middle ages often gave a present of a huge salmon to distinguished visitors. But the recipe can be used for any kind of big fish—halibut, cod or hake, and

9

it certainly gives character to some of the less interesting kinds of fish.

Since all salt-water fish has to be imported, no very distinctive recipes for it have developed. There are excellent, if a little expensive, fish from the lakes and rivers, however, the "ombres chevaliers" of the Lake of Geneva, and the Zugerrötel of Zoug. Pike is a favourite, both in French Switzerland (brochet) and in the east. Sandre (Zander) is another very good fish, the fillets of perch are a speciality of the Lake of Geneva, while the féra (Felchen in Eastern Switzerland) is extremely delicate, if slightly less exciting.

And finally, we come to the sausage. This figures very largely indeed in the Swiss menu, and there are countless varieties of it. There is the famous *Bratwurst,* which is made of veal, and is much less highly spiced than the pork sausage. The latter has a special form in the canton of Vaud (Waadtländer Bratwurst in Eastern Switzerland) which is very good indeed.

The smoked sausages of French Switzerland are mostly very good—have a try at saucisse aux choux or au foie, or simply a Vaud sausage with leeks. There is also an excellent Neuchatel sausage, more shapely than that of Vaud and a little finer in texture. Berne has its famous tongue sausage, which normally forms part of that fine dish, Bernerplatte (p. 37), and the Ticino has its salami. But to end this brief chronicle on the highest note, let those who travel in the Grisons try to find a Beinwurst, the queen of sausages. Bein is the Swiss for bone, and the peculiarity of this sausage is that whole lumps of delicious meat are stuffed into it including the bone. To eat a Beinwurst after a long and exhausting tramp brings beatitude. Let any man who questions anything Swiss

—democracy, neutrality, equality—go tired and hungry to an inn and find a Beinwurst. He will emerge a devout believer.

A note on the use of these recipes. They are not intended to teach people how to cook. Any housewife who has cooked for her family for years will know by instinct how much to take of things, and in a good many of the recipes, no quantities are given for that reason. They are only given where proportions are important. Swiss cookery is never finicking, and judgment must often take the place of exact instructions.

Mary Hottinger

Weights and Measures

The English system of weights and measures has been used throughout.

1 in.	=	25	millimeters
1 oz.	=	28	grammes
1 lb.	=	454	grammes
1 English pint	=	0.568	liters
1 American pint	=	0.473	liters
1 English quart	=	1.136	liters
1 American quart	=	0.946	liters

GENERAL

These few recipes are universal in Switzerland—one can't imagine the country without them.

Geröstete Mehlsuppe (Gravy Soup)

Make some fat very hot and put in five level tablespoonfuls of flour. Fry the flour on a gentle flame till it is a regular chestnut brown; (the beginner as a rule has her flour either too dark or too light; in the first case the soup is speckled and bitter, in the second, a particularly unappetizing drab colour). Now pour in a certain amount of cold liquid—water, stock, bouillon—and mix well, then add hot water or stock for the required amount of soup. It should boil at least 1 hour—the longer the better. Season before serving and add croutons or grated cheese. (This really delicious soup is the regular morning meal after carnival night at Basle, when the whole population has been in the streets all night. It is also served after big dances, but properly cooked, it is a meal in itself, and beats all dried soups hollow.)

Pot au Feu (Gesottenes Rindfleisch, Siedfleisch)

1½—2 lbs beef—not too fine a cut—with bones (brisket is very good). 5 pints water, salt, 1 small onion, a carrot, a stick of leek, a piece of celeriac, cabbage, tomatoes and other vegetables available.

Wash the bones and put them on to boil in cold water very slowly. Salt, then put in the meat and boil up again. Close the pot well and draw it a little to the side of the flame. Now add the vegetables and let the whole simmer on a very gentle flame for 2½ hours.

When ready, carve the meat in fairly thick slices, strew it with fine salt, pour a little of the liquor over it and garnish it with the vegetables. Gherkins, radishes or grated horseradish are also served.

(This dish, which is really very good, might be called the Swiss Housewife's Delight. It is very often made on Saturday, when the whole place is cleaned from top to bottom, and as it cooks away by itself and doesn't use up pans, it is very popular).

Geschnetzeltes Kalbfleisch (Emincé de Veau)

(This dish, which is a great favourite, depends on the chopping of the meat. It is cut, either by hand or by machine, into tiny squares about ⅛ in. thick—i. e. it is *not* minced. Since nothing is wasted, it is quite profitable.) Sauté a finely chopped onion in hot fat (still better, butter). Add the meat (4 ozs per serving) and steam on a hot flame till it has lost all red colour. Add a little more butter, season and serve with risotto or rösti. Some lemon juice improves the flavour.

14

Rösti (Swiss Fried Potatoes)

Cook potatoes in their jackets and peel them at once. Cut them in fine slices or rice them. Heat up plenty of butter or lard, add the potatoes and a little salt, and fry on a hot flame, turning all the time, till they are golden-brown. Now lower the flame, press the potatoes down and leave them for another few minutes till a golden crust forms underneath. Turn out so that the crust is uppermost. A finely chopped onion may be added.

Spaetzli (Knoepfli)

For 4 servings take rather less than 1 lb. flour, 1 teaspoon-ful salt, 1—2 eggs and 1 or 2 cups half milk, half water. Warm the milk and water and stir into the flour to make a thick batter. Add the eggs and beat the batter till bubbles form. Now drop the batter bit by bit from the point of a spoon into simmering salted water, or shred it with a knife from a flat plate or hand board. When the spaetzli rise to the top, remove from the water with a wire ladle and serve on a hot dish with butter, fried bread-crumbs or a smother of onions. They can also be served in layers with cheese between.

(Spaetzli are generally served with some kind of game or stew.)

Minestrone
Ticino

Soak some haricot beans overnight. Dice small quantities of any vegetable in season—carrots, turnips, celery, and so on; in winter, potatoes and cabbage can be used. The greater the variety of vegetables, the better the minestrone. Fry a little garlic in olive oil and add the diced vegetables. (For those not partial either to olive oil or garlic, diced bacon does very well.) Leave the vegetables to steam, adding a little water from time to time. Meanwhile, cook the beans till tender in another pan—fresh ones can be used in summer. Half an hour before serving, add the beans to the other vegetables with enough water to make a *thick* soup. Twenty minutes before serving throw in a handful of rice.

(Minestrone is a meal in itself, but one of the pitfalls for a small family is that it is very easy to make too much of it, especially if a large number of vegetables is available. The amounts used should therefore be calculated carefully. It can be heated up, but the family tends to get peevish the fourth time.)

Zuppa del paese
Ticino

Put a serving of hot stock or bouillon into small aluminium or other saucepans, one pan for each person. Add in each saucepan a slice of bread fried in fresh butter with one or two eggs on it, a small spoonful of tomato purée or gravy, and cover the whole with grated parmesan. Put the saucepan in a hot oven, and when the whites of the eggs have set, bring the soup to table. (Picturesque.)

Bulbura
Ticino

Peel and remove seeds from 4 lbs pumpkin. Cook in water; when soft, pour off the water and mash the pulp thoroughly. Add a little milk, a spoonful of flour, a knob of butter, salt and some cooked beans. Cook for half an hour, stirring frequently.

Broth
Schwyz

Melt a piece of butter in a deep frying-pan, add a spoonful of cream and fry 5—6 heaped-up tablespoonfuls of flour dark brown in this mixture. Then add boiling water and salt and boil thoroughly. The proportion of flour and butter should be such that the flour forms lumps, large and small.

Velouté
St. Gall

Boil up some stock or bouillon, stir in a little thickening of milk and flour and boil up again. Beat up a few eggs with cream in the tureen and pour in the boiling liquid very slowly, stirring continuously.

Busegga (Tripe Soup)
Ticino

Try out $1/4$ lb. bacon fat. When golden brown, add a little butter and steam the following ingredients in it: 1 finely chopped onion, a taste of garlic, a piece each of leek, celery, parsley and carrot, savory (the herb, not the angels on horseback), some shelled beans and 3—4 tomatoes. Pour not too much water over and cook for $1^1/2$ hours. 20 minutes before serving add 1 lb. cooked, finely shredded tripe and diced potatoes. Serve with grated cheese.

Milk Brose
Schwyz

Dice the necessary quantity of bread and fry it, add $1/2$ cup of water and $1/2$ cup of milk, and boil up. When ready, cover with a smother of fried onions.

CHEESE DISHES

Cheese Soup
Einsiedeln, Schwyz

Get a thoroughly crusty French loaf, cut it into fairly big slices, salt it, pour water over and leave till the bread has soaked up the water. Now melt a dessertspoonful of butter in a saucepan and add the soaked bread, mashing it with the potato masher. Boil up, stirring all the time, and adding gradually 1/2 lb. of grated Gruyère cheese. Simmer for ten minutes. Before serving, cover with a smother of sautéd onions.

(This is really not a soup at all, but a dish which is often served in Lent with plain boiled potatoes.)

Cheese Soup
Glarus

1/4 lb. Gruyère cheese, 1 pint boiling water, 1/2 lb. thin slices of bread browned in oven, 1 oz. melted butter.
Grate the cheese and lay it in the bowl in alternating layers with the bread. Pour boiling water over and leave for 10 minutes. Meanwhile melt some butter in frying-pan, then press bread and cheese down firmly, pour off

superfluous water and cook in the butter, stirring all the time, till the whole becomes glazed, i. e. till the fat has come out of the cheese. Serve very hot.

Another method—do not stir the bread and cheese in the pan but make a pancake of it. In this case a good deal more butter must be used.

Cheese Tart
Einsiedeln, Schwyz

Line a medium-sized sandwich-tin with unsweetened scone dough. Spread the following mixture on it: $1^1/_2$ lbs cheese (if possible, half dry and half creamy) finely shredded, 5 eggs, 3 chopped and fried onions, $1^1/_2$ cups milk, 4 spoonfuls water and a pinch of salt. Bake for half an hour in a moderate oven.

Cheese Tart and Spiced Potatoes
The potatoes are called "suri Gumeli"
Schwyz

Line a sandwich tin with bread dough (scone dough made without butter will do, but ordinary pastry should never be used). For a tin about 12 ins. in diameter, grate 1 lb. Gruyère cheese, chop and fry one large onion in plenty of fat, beat 2 eggs, then thoroughly mix cheese, onion, eggs and a pinch of salt, adding a little milk if the mixture is too stiff. It should be spread about an inch thick. Bake in a hot oven and serve very hot. In the canton of Schwyz, it is usually served with *"suri Gumeli"* (it is unnecessary to know how to pronounce this in order to appreciate it) i.e. steamed potatoes cut in thick slices and spiced with bay, cloves and a little vinegar.

Cheese Wreath
Appenzell

14 ozs flour, a cup of milk, $1/2$ lb. strong cheese, 3 eggs, a pinch each of salt and carbonate of soda, fat for frying. Mix the ingredients into a thick batter and beat till bubbles form. Put plenty of fat into the frying-pan, and when it is quite hot, put the batter into it in a ring of little heaps right round the edge of the pan. Add a second row "staggered" with the first. Leave the middle empty. The heaps should touch, but not run into each other. When golden-brown on one side, turn over (if you can) and fry on other. Cover for a minute or two to prevent hardening and serve with stewed dried fruit, vegetables or salad.
(Delicious, but not for the unskilled cook or the unsteady hand.)

Cheese Flan
Appenzell

Filling: $1/2$ lb. flour, 1 cup cream, fresh or sour, a little milk, 1 large sliced onion, $1/2$ lb. Gruyère cheese, 1 egg, 1 lb. short pastry.
For the filling make a very thick batter of the flour, milk and cream, add the onions, the cheese in fine parings, a little salt and the egg. Mix well. Line a sandwich tin with the pastry, spread the mixture on and bake.

Ramekins
Neuchatel

Enough short pastry for 16 individual ramekins: $1/2$ lb. flour, 1 cup cream off scalded milk or 2 ozs butter, a pinch of salt. Roll out very thin, and after leaving in a cool place for half an hour, line ramekins. Mix $1/2$ lb. Gruyère cheese with 2 eggs and 1 cup of milk. Fill ramekins half full with mixture. Bake in hot oven and serve very hot. The same recipe can be used for a single large cheese flan.

Ramekins
Vaud

(6 servings) $1/4$ lb. cheese, 1 oz. butter, 1 spoonful flour, seasoning, 3—4 eggs, $1/2$ lb. short pastry, a little cream. Mix the eggs thoroughly with the flour, cream, butter, seasoning and 2 ozs grated cheese. Cut 2 ozs cheese in small dice and add, butter ramekins and line with pastry. Bake light brown. Fill with mixture and put back in oven. Increase heat very slowly. When the ramekins are golden brown, serve immediately.

Raclette
Valais

Take a large piece of creamy white cheese. Make a wood or charcoal fire. Cut the cheese in two and toast the two halves over each other in front of it. As soon as the cheese runs, scrape the liquid part on to a hot plate. Hold cheese to the fire again and repeat till all guests have been served. To be eaten with boiled potatoes.

(This remarkably good recipe may recall to an older generation some of the more joyous flights of the Week-end Book, but if no wood or charcoal is available, a gas fire has its potentialities.)

Fondue
Neuchatel

For each serving, 1/4 lb. Gruyère cheese and 1/2 gill Fendant or other white wine—dry if possible. Rub an earthenware casserole with garlic. Warm the wine in the casserole, add the cheese, finely pared, and bring to the boil, stirring all the time. Add 1—2 teaspoonfuls of potato flour mixed with a little wine and a dessertspoonful of kirsch (if you can get it; a dry sherry sometimes does the trick). In 3—4 minutes the fondue will have thickened and can be brought to table. Put on a chafing dish or spirit lamp to keep at boiling point. Each person dips pieces of bread on a fork in the fondue, stirring each time. It is eaten straight from the casserole.

Fondue
Geneva

Take the yolks of 8 eggs and mix in a saucepan with 1/2 lb. grated cheese, pepper, grated nutmeg and a pinch of salt. Add, bit by bit, 5 ozs butter, stirring continuously over gentle flame without boiling. When the mixture thickens, add half a glass of cream, stir a little longer and serve in a deep dish surrounded by slices of fried bread. This type of fondue is generally eaten with noodles.

Gratin montagnard
Vaud

1 quart milk, 4 eggs, $1/2$ lb. cheese. Butter a pie dish. Warm milk in a saucepan, add a knob of butter and a pinch of salt. Then stir in 2 dessertspoonfuls of semolina. When the mixture thickens, add cheese finely pared and stir till cheese is melted. Leave the whole to cool, then add the yolks of the eggs, fold in the whipped whites, fill a buttered sandwich-tin and bake about 40 minutes till golden-brown.

MEATLESS DISHES

Maluns
Grisons

Mix 2 parts of mashed potatoes with 1 part flour and salt. Melt some butter very hot in the frying-pan, work in the mixture, turning it over and over till it falls into crumbs. When these are golden-brown, but are still soft ($^3/_4$ hour), the maluns is ready. Before serving, work in a piece of fresh butter. Maluns is specially good with coffee, and is therefore a favourite supper-dish in the Grisons.

Potato Whacks
Grisons

Peel and grate 5—6 fairly large potatoes. Add 2 eggs and 2—3 spoonfuls of flour and mix thoroughly. Before frying, work in 2 spoonfuls of hot dripping or fat. Fry in spoonfuls in deep fat till golden-brown.

Gnocchi
Ticino

Boil and mash 1 lb. potatoes. Mix in 2 ozs of flour and a pinch of salt. Work well. Drop spoonfuls into boiling salted water. Strain, pour melted butter over and strew with grated cheese. Part spinach and part potatoes can also be used.

Matafan
Fribourg

Dip thin slices of bread in hot milk. Make a batter of flour, milk, eggs, sugar and salt, whipping the whites of the eggs stiff and folding them in last. Line a greased tin with the bread, pour the batter over and bake in a moderate oven. When ready, turn out on to a dish and serve in slices.

Maize Pudding (Maisturta)
Nidwalden

This is generally made in winter when the stove is on (not the gas stove, of course). Boil $1^1/_2$ pints of water with a little milk, sugar and salt. Add currants or sultanas, then pour in enough maize mixed with semolina to thicken when boiled. Work in a little butter, spread the boiled mixture on a greased fireproof dish and bake in a quick oven. This will make five servings. It is generally eaten with tea as a midday meal.

Potato Cake (Kartoffelhurtä)
Nidwalden

Boil a number of small potatoes in their jackets, peel and mash. Mix with a little flour and salt and fill a shallow, greased piedish with them. Cover with sliced apples or rashers of bacon and bake in a quick oven.

Potato Cake
Zoug

Boil and mash potatoes (leftovers can also be used). Cover a fireproof dish with dots of butter, put in the potatoes and smooth flat with a spoon. Now mix thoroughly 2 eggs, 1 cup cream, 1/2 lb. grated Gruyère cheese, or half Gruyère and half Parmesan, pour the mixture over the potatoes and bake 20 minutes to 1/2 hour.

Broken Pancake (Kohlermus)
Schwyz

Beat 12 spoonfuls of flour, 1/2 teaspoonful of salt and 4—5 eggs to a thick batter. Fry, breaking up all the time with the pancake-turner, till the pieces are golden-brown all over.

Broken Pancake (Cholermus)
Unterwalden

Mix cream, or milk and cream, an egg or two if possible, and white flour to a thick batter. Pour into fairly hot butter, and fry golden-brown, cutting up the batter as it fries and turning the pieces. This rather indigestible dish is a great favourite with the dairymen on the summer pastures in the Alps.

Pancake Dabs (Pfueserli)
Schaffhouse

Melt 1 oz. butter in 1 gill warm milk and stir in 3—4 spoonfuls of flour to make a batter. Before frying, fold in the stiffly beaten whites of 2—3 eggs. Fry in pieces the size of a walnut in very hot fat. This is an excellent garnish to vegetables.

Onion Tart (Bölledünne)
Schaffhouse

Line a large sandwich tin with short pastry. Peel and shred 2 lbs onions and fry in lard till glazed. Spread on pastry. Beat 2 eggs with some milk or cream, season and pour over onions. Bake in a hot oven and serve very hot.

Potato Pears
Lucerne

Soak dried pears for 1—2 hours in lukewarm water. Meanwhile peel three times the amount of potatoes, cut them in small pieces about the size of a walnut (the pieces should be rather irregular) and pour cold water over them. Put 1—2 spoonfuls of fat in a saucepan, sauté one large sliced onion in it, drain the potatoes and put them in. Salt, add the pears in the water they have been soaked in, nearly enough to cover, and stew for about 40 minutes till the whole is tender and juicy. It is served with beef and pork. A little still cider or 1—2 spoonfuls of honey are an improvement. When in season, fresh pears or apples can be used, but should be slightly sweetened before cooking.

Gonterser Bock
Grisons

(It is quite impossible to devise a worthy name for this in English. The native name can be learned with practice.)

Make a batter of flour, 1 egg, milk and salt. Dip a hard-boiled egg in and fry at once in hot butter. As soon as it is light brown, dip again in the batter and fry, repeating the process till the whole is a large ball. (This is extremely nourishing, and it is not necessary to allow one egg per serving.)

Potato and Apple Mash (Krusi or Funggi)
Soleure

Parboil some potatoes cut in pieces in slightly salted water, drain and cover with sliced apples. Add a little water and sugar and cook potatoes and apples together till tender. Add a thickening of 1 teaspoonful of flour blended with milk or cream—about $3/4$ of a cupful. Now mash the whole with the potato-masher, boil slowly on a gentle flame for 5 minutes, stirring to prevent burning. This mash is particularly good with stews.

Polenta
Valais

Boil 3 pints of water with a teaspoonful of salt. Pour in about 1 lb. maize flour and cook $1/2 — 3/4$ hours on a gentle flame, stirring frequently with a wooden spoon. When the polenta is ready, it can be used in various ways.

1) Butter a fireproof dish. Take spoonfuls of the polenta and lay them side by side in the dish with a slice of cheese on each spoonful. Cover with white sauce, strew with grated cheese and breadcrumbs, and bake $1/4$ hour in a hot oven.

2) Pare and cut up 1—2 apples and steam slightly in a piece of butter. Cut the polenta into pieces, add to the apples and fry till ready.

3) Cut squares out of the polenta, lay on a butted baking-tin, strew with 2—3 handfuls of grated cheese and bake golden-brown in a hot oven.

4) Sauté a finely chopped onion in a great deal of butter, put the polenta, still hot, on to a deep dish, pour over it the butter and onions and serve very hot.

Spaetzli with Beans
Thurgovie

Make some spaetzli. In the meantime, steam beans till tender in a little butter and salted water. Put a layer of

PUBLICATIONS IN ENGLISH

Hans Huber
HOW SWITZERLAND IS GOVERNED
sFr. 4.—

This booklet has also been published
in Spanish under the title
COMO SE GOBIERNA SUIZA
sFr. 4.—

and in German under the title
WIE DIE SCHWEIZ REGIERT WIRD
sFr. 4.—

B. Bradfield
A POCKET HISTORY OF
SWITZERLAND
with Historical Outline and Guide
sFr. 3.60

W. Hofer
NEUTRALITY AS THE PRINCIPLE
OF SWISS FOREIGN POLICY
sFr. 3.70

Collected by Helen Guggenbühl
THE SWISS COOKERY BOOK
Recipes from all cantons
sFr. 4.80

SCHWEIZER SPIEGEL VERLAG ZÜRICH 1

spaetzli into a piedish, then a layer of beans, and repeat till beans and spaetzli are used up, the top layer being spaetzli. Fry finely sliced onions in butter and pour them over the spaetzli. In winter, this dish can be made with sterilized beans.

Spinach Tart
Argovie

Line a sandwich tin with puff or short pastry and cover with the following mixture—steam finely chopped spinach in dripping, add 2—3 beaten eggs and a little cream. Cover with some diced bacon. Bake in moderate oven.

Potatoes and Dab (Stupfete)
Thurgovie

This excellent dish is made in autumn, at the time of what is known in Scotland as the tattie-lifting. Take a three-legged pot which will stand on the fire, pour in three spoonfuls of olive oil (or butter), five of vinegar, two chopped onions, salt and pepper. Bring the pot to table very hot, and each person dips his potatoes, which have been boiled in their jackets, into it.

Onion Rolls
Thurgovie

Work some butter into scone dough, roll it out about $1/2$ in. thick, cover densely with raw, salted onions, make little rolls and bake.

31

These rolls are made in Weinfelden on the night on which the Black Death is commemorated. The children run from house to house singing, and gather afterwards round onion rolls and cider.

Spinach Turnovers (Krautkräpfli)
Grisons

Make a noodle dough of flour, a cupful of lukewarm milk and water, 1 egg and salt. Work well and put aside for 1—2 hours. Meanwhile make a filling of cooked spinach mixed with finely chopped onion, parsley, chives, 1—2 leaves of mint, and breadcrumbs, the whole fried in butter and saisoned with salt and nutmeg. The filling should be as dry as possible and chilled before use so that it does not break the dough.

Roll out the dough very thin, cover half with little balls of filling. Fold the other half over and press carefully down between the balls. Now cut out the balls and cook in boiling water like spaetzli, then serve covered with butter and grated cheese.

Onion Salad
Neuchatel

Cut the onions in horizontal slices $1/2$ in. thick and fry light brown in plenty of fat. Remove them from the fat (which can be used again) and mix with salt, 1 spoonful of flour and 2 spoonfuls of vinegar. Onion salad is always served with boiled potatoes.

Tuerkenribel
Glarus

4 servings. 1 lb. maize, $^1/_2$ lb. flour and a little salt. Mix
with boiling milk and leave to stand for an hour or two.
Then fry in butter over a gentle flame. While stirring,
add more butter and if necessary a little milk to prevent
drying. Delicious little lumps form, and the dish is ready
in about $^3/_4$ hour.

Wehntal Maize
Aargau

Stir $^3/_4$—1 lb. of maize into 3 quarts of boiling water
till it thickens. Meanwhile make croutons of bread and
mix in the maize. When ready, cover with hot melted
butter.
Very good with or without stewed fruit—a nourishing
supper dish.

Flugets
Glarus

Make a stiff spaetzli batter. Mix in enough chopped
cooked spinach or greens to make the batter bright green.
Have ready a saucepan of boiling water and make spaetzli
as on p. 15. Serve with a smother of onions or breadcrumbs fried in butter, or butter and grated cheese. These
flugets are also good with minced meat mixed into them,
or again can be left to cool and then fried as a kind of
pancake.

Potato Cake (Ofentürli)
Schwyz

Boil and mash 2 lbs of potatoes, work in 4 ozs of flour,
$1/2$ lb. butter and a little salt. Well grease a medium-
sized sandwich tin and fill with the mixture. Dot over
the $1/2$ lb. of butter and bake in a fairly quick oven.
Serve with coffee and milk.

MEAT

Liver Skewers
Zurich

Cut calf or beef liver into thumb-size pieces. Wrap each piece first in a fresh sage-leaf, then in a piece of veal caul and thread on to a very fine wooden skewer or a knitting-needle, 5—6 to each skewer. Brown in a frying-pan with butter and onions, preferably covered, till the liver is cooked. The best vegetable for these skewers is beans.

(Very thin half-rashers of bacon can be used instead of the veal caul, but in that case the onions should be omitted.)

Zurich Hotpot

Ingredients: 3/4 lb. pork, 3/4 lb. cabbage, 1 lb. potatoes, 4 carrots, 1 onion, 1 teaspoonful salt, pepper, water.

Cut the pork into stewing pieces, shred the cabbage, dice the potatoes, slice the carrots and the onions. Put in a saucepan with a close-fitting lid in the following order: meat, salt, pepper, onion, cabbage, salt, pepper, onion and finally meat. Add water to half-way up and leave to steam over a gentle flame, without stirring, for 1 1/2—2 hours.

Dried Chestnuts and Smoked Pork
Uri

Soak the chestnuts overnight. The following morning, simmer in slightly salted water with a piece of smoked pork — ¹/₂ lb. pork to 1 lb. of chestnuts. This requires long, slow cooking (2—3 hours).

Cabbage Hotpot
Uri

Cut mutton in stewing pieces, sear in hot fat, add shredded cabbage, a little salt and a little water. Steam until meat is tender and the cabbage yellow. This is the staple dish at the great annual fair in the canton of Uri.

Turnips and Pork
Baar, canton of Zoug

(This is a special dish for the annual fair in November.) Pare 6—8 turnips, according to size, cut in quarters and boil for ¹/₂ hour. Pour away the water, add fresh boiling water and boil again for ¹/₂ hour. Meanwhile brown 2 lbs of salt pork (neck or loin) in a little fat, add it to the turnips and cook till the meat is tender. Half an hour before serving mash the turnips, make a thickening of 2 spoonfuls of flour with cream or milk, add to the mashed turnips and finish cooking. The whole should be golden-brown—i. e. it may be allowed to stick to the pan a little, though not to burn. (These *räben* are larger and coarser than turnips, but turnips can be used in the recipe.)

Berner Platte
Berne

(It would be a shame to deprive this noble dish of its name, which it bears throughout Switzerland.)
Cook pigs' trotters, ears and tongue till tender. Sauerkraut is cooked with a piece of bacon, ham and a smoked sausage (in Switzerland, of course, the Bernese kind). The bacon and sausage will be ready in about an hour. Keep them warm and continue cooking the rest. When ready, serve with the sauerkraut in the middle of the dish, surrounded by the sliced bacon, ham, sausage, pigs' trotters, ears etc.

Scaloppine
Ticino

Beat veal cutlets very thin and turn in flour. Fry lightly on both sides, add a small glass of white wine and leave for five minutes. Salt just before serving. Dish up on a bed of risotto. Add to the liquor in the frying-pan the yolk of an egg and the juice of half a lemon. Stir this gravy well, without allowing it to boil, and pour over the meat very hot. Serve at once.

Stuffato alla Chiassese
Ticino

Lard a piece of beef with bacon and garlic, dredge with flour and brown in butter and chopped onions. As soon as it is brown all over, add half a glass of wine and, if necessary, a little water. About 3/4 hour before serving, add a few potatoes and tomatoes cut in pieces. Carve before bringing to table and dish up with the tomatoes and potatoes.

Fricandeau à la Genevoise

2 lbs veal, 2 ozs lean bacon, $1^1/_2$ ozs fat bacon, 1 oz. dripping, 1 oz. flour, salt, a mirepoix (according to Ambrose Heath equal parts of carrot, onion and celery), $1/_2$ pint of water and a small cup of white wine.

Make a hole in the meat and fill it with the lean bacon. Lard the outside with the fat bacon. Roll the meat in flour and place in hot dripping in a casserole with the larded side up. Brown the meat thoroughly in the oven. Now add the mirepoix, water and wine. Cook for 2 hours, basting frequently. Add salt $1/_4$ hour before serving. Remove meat from casserole, add 1 gill of cream to gravy and heat well without allowing to boil.

Stuffed Cabbage (Kabis-Buenteli)
Zoug

Parboil a whole cabbage. Separate the leaves. On each leaf place a spoonful of good sausage meat, roll up and fry brown all over, basting all the time. After removing the rolls from the pan, boil up the gravy with a little stock or bouillon and pour it over them. These rolls can also be made into a vegetarian dish by leaving out the meat and filling with soaked bread, egg, chopped parsley and chives, flavoured with a little marjoram and onion.

Ofentori
Unterwalden

Boil and mash potatoes, add salt, pepper, grated nutmeg, a little milk or cream, 1 or 2 eggs and a large quantity of diced bacon. Mix well, fill into a well-greased piedish, strew the top with more diced bacon and bake in a hot oven.

Lucerne Pasty

Shell: Make a dough with 2 lbs flour, 3 eggs and water. When well worked, roll out and spread 2 lbs of fresh butter on it. Fold in three and roll out again. Repeat twice, leaving the dough to stand, if possible, for $1/4$ hour between rollings. Cut a large round out of the dough and place on a greased baking-tin. Lay a strip of pastry 1 in. wide all round the edge and brush over with yolk of egg. In the middle, put a crumpled paper with a clean table napkin on it. Now make a lid from the remains of the dough, 1 in. bigger all round than the bottom, put over table napkin, brush the whole with yolk of egg and fix a round of pastry cut out with a small wine-glass to the middle of the lid. Bake in a very hot oven. When cold, carefully cut a round out of the top and remove the paper and napkin. Now fill your pasty—stewed veal, and, as desired, sultanas, sweetbreads, brains or mushrooms, and heat up in the oven. As a rule, a sauce is handed separately.

In many parts of Switzerland, January 2nd, St. Bertold's day, is an occasion of great feasting in the guilds, and this pasty is a feature of such meals at Lucerne. It is rather picturesque for any but Swiss conditions.

Lettuce and Bacon
Neuchatel

Wash 5—6 heads of lettuce whole. Cook in a saucepan with a little lard, salt, pepper, a little warm water, a Neuchatel sausage (any good smoked sausage will do) and some bacon. After $3/4$ hour take out the sausage, and put in a warm place, leaving the rest to cook for another hour. Beans are also cooked in this way in the canton of Neuchatel.

Tripe
Neuchatel

Wash the raw tripe and boil it slowly for 4 hours with the ingredients generally used for a clear soup, and, if desired, 1—2 pigs' trotters. Serve with a vinaigrette of oil, vinegar, mustard, pepper and plenty of chopped onions.

Tripe
Valais

Cut the tripe into thin strips and cover with salted water. Make a sauce of butter, flour, chopped onions, bouillon cubes, 2 tomatoes or tomato purée, salt and pepper. Simmer on a gentle flame for 3 hours. Before serving, add a little cream, $1/2$ glass of vinegar and some grated cheese.

Steamed Mutton and Potatoes
Grisons

Heat some lard in a frying-pan and fry the mutton cut
in small pieces (breast by preference) with a sliced onion.
Then put it into a casserole, pour hot water over it and
add a bay-leaf, salt and pepper. After an hour, add raw
potatoes cut in pieces. The potatoes must not crumble,
and care must be taken that the liquor does not boil
away, so that there is enough gravy left for serving.

Liver Spaetzli
Thurgovie

1 lb. minced liver, 1 lb. flour, and 2 eggs beaten with a
little water added. Mix well. Make like plain spaetzli
(see p. 15) and serve with potato salad.

Salmon
Basle

(For Swiss fish in general, see Introduction, though, as mentioned in the Introduction, the recipe can be used for any large fish. This noble dish is here given for purely picturesque reasons.)

For 6 servings take 3 lbs of salmon. After cleaning and scaling, cut into slices $1/2$ in. thick, dry with a clean cloth (do not soak or wash), rub with salt and pepper, dredge with flour, lay the slices side by side in the frying-pan and fry quickly golden-brown on both sides, turning carefully to keep slices whole. When the fish begins to come away from the bones, arrange the slices on a dish and put in a warm place. Add a little more butter to what is left in the pan, fry 1—2 shredded onions in it and pour over the slices of salmon. Dissolve the glaze in the pan with a little bouillon or gravy and pour over fish.

SWEETS AND CAKES

Sugar Tart (Zuckerwähe)
Zurich

Line a sandwich tin with short pastry, break 4 eggs on to it, whisk them lightly with a spoon and dot over with 2 ozs of butter. Then bake. When ready, serve sprinkled with $^{1}/_{2}$ cup of castor sugar mixed with a little cinnamon, and with more dots of butter, especially in places which have dried and blistered.

Bilberry Fool
Berne

2 lbs bilberries (whortleberries or blaeberries) 2 ozs sugar, 4 ozs diced bread, $^{1}/_{2}$ pint milk. Pound the berries in a bowl. Fry the diced bread in hot fat and mix it into the berries with the sugar. Add the cold milk and mix well.

Castagnaccio
Ticino

5 ozs chestnuts, 4 ozs sugar, 1$^{1}/_{2}$ ozs butter, 5 eggs, 1 gill milk, 2 spoonfuls maraschino (or dry sherry), vanilla and sugar. Boil the chestnuts in water for 5 minutes — just long enough to be able to shell and peel them. Then cook till tender in the milk, press through a sieve and mix with the sugar, the melted butter, the maraschino or sherry and the vanilla. Finally add the yolks of the eggs and the whites beaten to froth. Bake in a buttered dish and dust over with fine sugar before serving.

Zabaione
Ticino

4 yolks of egg, 4 dessertspoonfuls of castor sugar, 4 of water, 4 of malaga (or 8 of ordinary white wine). Mix well. Put on fire and stir the whole time. Just before boiling, the zabaione rises. Remove it immediately from the fire and set aside to cool. Then stir in a dessertspoonful of milk or cream.

Elderberry Mush
Toggenburg, St. Gall

Mix 1—1$^{1}/_{2}$ ozs of fresh butter with a cup of milk and cream and a dessertspoonful of flour to a smooth batter, add 1$^{1}/_{2}$—2 lbs of elderberries and cook the whole for $^{1}/_{4}$ hour over a gentle flame. Another method is to keep the butter till the mush is ready, then pour it over very hot. It is usually served with coffee.

Apple Fritters (Pfnutli)
Basle

Cut some tart apples into pieces the size of a walnut, heat some sugar in wine, carefully blend the sugared wine with 6 spoonfuls of flour, break 3 eggs into the mixture and stir well. Dip the apples in the batter so that it quite covers them and fry in spoonfuls golden-brown in hot butter. On taking them out of the pan, roll immediately in fine sugar.

Sèche au Vin
Geneva

Line a shallow tin with short pastry and prick well with a fork. Then cover with a layer of castor sugar mixed with a little flour. Pour over white wine mixed with cinnamon and dot with butter. The wine must not overflow. Bake in a hot oven.

Apfelbröisi
Argovie

Fry a plateful of thin slices of stale bread in butter, stirring well. Add the same weight of pared and finely sliced apples and steam till the apples are tender. Add sugar and sultanas to taste. This is a great favourite with children.

Horsehoofs (Strüzels)
Grisons

1 lb. flour, 2 eggs, 2 ozs butter, 3 ozs sugar, 1 oz. sultanas, $1/2$ pint milk and a tablespoonful of baking-powder. Work well together, then take spoonfuls and shape them into horsehoofs. They are fried in deep lard, not too hot, till golden-brown on both sides and dusted over with sugar. Eat cold or hot—preferably with coffee.

Cream Tart
Appenzell

$1/2$ pint of cream, 3 heaped spoonfuls of flour (if the cream is thin, a little more), a pinch of salt, if liked, a spoonful of coriander and aniseed and 1 egg. Mix well, and spread over scone dough in a sandwich tin. Bake till dough is cooked.

Sage Fritters
Zurich

$1/2$ lb. of flour, a pinch of salt, $1/2$ pint of wine (or beer), 2 eggs, fresh sage leaves, fat for frying.
Mix the salt into the flour and stir with the slightly warmed wine or beer and the yolks of the eggs to a smooth, firm batter. Beat the whites to a stiff froth and fold into batter. Dip sage leaves by the stem into the batter, fry in deep fat, then dust over with sugar.
(These sage fritters are here treated as a sweet, but they can be served with lean cold ham—omitting the sugar, of course—with great success.)

46

Cherry Bunches
Argovie

Tie cherries in bunches by the stalks, five or six to a
bunch, dip in batter and fry in deep fat. After frying,
roll in sugar and cinnamon.

Carnival Pancakes
Zurich

1 cupful of cream, 2 ozs of melted fresh butter and
enough hot milk to make a firm dough. Turn the mixture
into 2^1/$_2$ lbs of flour with a teaspoonful of salt to the lb.,
work as quickly as possible into dough, then cover to
prevent warmth escaping. Roll out ^{1}/$_2$ in. thick, cut into
small squares and fry in hot butter.

If the fritters are not eaten up at once, they should be
put away in a jar or enamel pot with a heavy lid. In this
way they will remain soft. Exposure to air makes them
hard and brittle.

Carnival Cakes (Eieröhrli)
Zurich

8 small eggs, ^{1}/$_2$ cup of cream, a pinch of salt, 3 tablespoonfuls of pounded sugar, 1 oz. of fresh butter, melted.
Beat well for ^{1}/$_4$ hour, slowly adding enough flour to
make a dough, then leave standing for ^{1}/$_4$ hour. Cut out
balls about as big as a small apple, roll out as thin as possible, then pull very carefully by hand until they are as
thin as tissue paper (this is essential). Fry in butter in a

small pan and sprinkle immediately with fine sugar. They will keep for weeks.

(These carnival cakes can be seen in piles in every confectioners' window in Zurich at carnival time.)

Waffles
Zurich

Mix 6 eggs, 6 ozs flour, 1 pint milk and 1 cup fresh cream. Add the grated rind of a lemon, mix in 1/4 lb. of melted butter and a little salt and leave dough to stand for 1/2 hour. Grease waffle iron and bake on both sides.

Krapfen
Berne

Pastry: 2 lbs flour, 7 ozs butter or margarine, a good half pint of milk, salt.

Filling: 4 lbs dried pears, 3 lbs walnuts. Wash pears and simmer till tender, then put through the mincer with the nuts. If necessary, add a little sugar.

Melt the fat in milk and water with a little salt, then pour into a bowl to cool. Add the flour slowly and work in. Roll out this dough very thin (in the original recipe it says 1/8 in.) cover half with the filling, fold the other half over and run round the edge with the pastry cutter. Now press into squares with the sharp edge of a ruler and cut out the squares with the pastry cutter. Fry in deep fat till golden-brown. In order to prevent bursting while frying, it is advisable to leave the krapfen in a cool place for a few hours beforehand.

Scrambled Pancakes
Berne

10 ozs flour, 2 eggs, 2 ozs butter, $1/2$ pint white wine or still cider, a few drops of kirsch. (Kirsch gives the best taste, but gin or dry sherry can also be used.)
Melt the butter and leave to cool down. Beat the eggs, then stir in the butter, wine and kirsch. Add flour and work well together. Form small balls and roll out to the size of a dinner plate. Fry in deep fat and strew with sugar.

Krapfen
St. Gall

1 lb. sugar, 3 eggs, the grated rind of a lemon (if possible, a dessertspoonful of orange-flower water) 1 lb. flour. Work into a dough, roll and cut in rounds.
Filling: $1/2$ lb. unblanched almonds, $1/2$ lb. sugar, $1^{1}/2$ teaspoonfuls cinnamon, $1/2$ teaspoonful grated nutmeg, $1/2$ teaspoonful crushed cloves. Mix well and moisten with a little milk.
Cover half of each round with filling and pinch edges together. Leave overnight in moderately warm place. Then warm (not heat) oven and bake in moderate heat, having first brushed the krapfen over with sugar melted in water.

Beignets de Bénichon
Fribourg

3 yolks of egg, 3 whole eggs, 2 ozs sugar, 2 teaspoonfuls kirsch, 1 gill fresh cream, flour, salt.

Beat the yolks and the whole eggs together for 20 minutes. Add the sugar, kirsch, salt and cream, then enough flour to make the dough stiff enough to work by hand. It should be kneaded on a floured board for 1/4 hour. Form into little balls, and leave them to stand for 2 hours. Then roll them out as thin as possible and fry them brown in butter. Dust fine sugar over them as soon as they are removed from the pan.

Gateau fribourgeois

Pastry: 1/2 lb. flour, 1/4 lb. butter, 6—8 spoonfuls salted water.

Filling: 1/2 lb. almonds, 1/4 lb. sugar, 1 gill water, 2 ozs butter, a pinch of salt.

First make pastry and leave to stand in a cool place for 1/4 hour. Blanch and pound almonds, then mix in a saucepan with the sugar, butter, water and salt over a hot flame until the mixture comes to the boil. Then remove and leave mixture to cool. Line a greased sandwich tin with the pastry, cover with the filling and ornament with a lattice-work of pastry brushed over with yolk of egg. In each of the lozenge-shaped spaces put a tiny piece of candied lemon peel. Bake in a hot oven.

Honey Tart
Unterwalden

Pastry: 1 quart of milk, 1/2 lb. sugar, 1 1/2 lbs honey, (or maple syrup), 1 1/2 ozs cinnamon, 1 oz aniseed, any other spices available, 2 ozs salt, flour to mix.

Filling: Brown or black breadcrumbs (stale), sugar, cinnamon, coriander, orange and lemon peel and some honey to prevent drying.

Roll out pastry, spread filling evenly over it, cover with pastry, press a mould on top, bake in a moderate oven. After baking, brush over with honey.

Wrinkled Jam Tarts
Schaffhouse

10 ozs flour, 2 eggs, 1/2 lb. butter, 3 spoonfuls sugar, a pinch of salt.

Knead all the ingredients into a round ball, cut it in 12 equal parts, roll out each part as thin as possible and leave to dry. Now lay one part on the pastry-board and brush about 1/8 of the surface with melted butter. Then lay a second part just to overlap the buttered part of the first, again brush 1/8 with melted butter and lay a third to overlap this. Continue till all 12 pieces are used up. Roll the whole up as tightly as possible and leave in a cool place overnight.

Without unrolling, cut slices 1 in. thick from the roll, and roll these out again very thin. When baked, the marks of the original layering will reappear. Cover half of each piece with jam, fold the other half over, pinch the edges together and bake in a moderate oven.

Pear Bread
Glarus

14 lbs of dried pears, 6—7 lbs of walnuts, $2^{1}/_2$ lbs of sultanas, 4—5 lbs of sugar, $^{1}/_2$ lb of cinnamon, 4—5 nutmegs, $^{1}/_2$ lb. candied orange peel, the peel of 1 lemon, 1 quart of rose-water, 1 pint kirsch, with a little wine if needed, 12 lbs of bread dough.

Cook the pears till tender, clean and chop finely. Divide the dough into two equal parts, knead the larger part into the pears, adding the other ingredients gradually. Roll out the other part of the dough, cut in pieces big enough to wrap round small loaves made of the mixture, which should be entirely covered. Prick a few holes in the top and bake in a hot oven.

(This recipe is given partly for the sake of local colour, and partly to enable the uninitiated to recognize this kind of loaf when they see it. It is golden-brown outside, black inside. It is said to date from the Napoleonic Wars, when there were plenty of pears, but little flour. It is still made in the quantities given above in many Glarus households, put aside, and brought out on special occasions.)

Uri Pasty

$1^{1}/_2$ lbs flour, $^{1}/_2$ lb butter, $^{1}/_2$ teaspoonful salt, $^{3}/_4$ lb. sugar, a small glass of brandy or dry sherry (the original recipe says marc), 1 egg and some still cider or water. Work these ingredients into a smooth dough and leave overnight. Then cut the dough into two parts and roll out. Spread one half with 2 ozs each of currants and sultanas sprinkled with sugar and cinnamon. Fit a strip of dough 1 in. wide round edge, then cover with the other half of the dough and fit another strip of pastry round the cover. Press down the edge all round with a fork and brush over the whole with yolk of egg. Bake in a hot oven.

Bernese Läckerli

1 lb. sugar, ½ lb. unblanched almonds, ½ lb. hazelnuts, 2 ozs flour, 1 teaspoonful cinnamon, 4 ozs orange peel, 1 tablespoonful honey, 4—5 whites of egg.

Mix all ingredients well, except eggs. Whisk the white of egg to a stiff froth and work with the mixture into a dough. Roll out ½ in. thick, flour the läckerli moulds and press into dough. Cut out cleanly and spread on a buttered baking-tin. Bake in a moderate oven and immediately on taking out, brush over with thin sugar glaze.

Honey Bread
Appenzell

1 lb. flour, 4 ozs sugar, ½ lb. honey (or maple syrup), 1 egg, cinnamon, pounded cloves and grated nutmeg, a tablespoonful baking-powder.

Dissolve the honey; mix the sugar, egg and a little milk very thoroughly, then work all the ingredients into a firm dough and leave to stand for a few hours. Roll out finger-thick, cut in rounds the size of a small plate, brush with milk and bake on a greased tin in a moderate oven.

Beavers
St. Gall

1 lb. honey (or maple syrup), $1/4$ lb. sugar, 1 lemon peel,
1 teaspoonful cinnamon, two pinches of pounded cloves,
2 of grated nutmeg, $1^{1}/4$ lbs flour, 3 dessertspoonfuls
rose-water, $1/2$ teaspoonful potash.

Boil the honey, then add the sugar, lemon peel, cinnamon, cloves and nutmeg. Sift the flour in gradually,
stirring all the time and add the potash dissolved in the
rose-water. Then place the dough on a floured pastry-
board, and knead, roll out $1/4$ in. thick and cut out in oblongs 2 in. by 1 in size. Leave them to dry overnight on
a floured board. Bake the next day in moderate heat on
a buttered or waxed tin. If desired, brush over while still
warm with melted syrup.

Lebkuchen
Lucerne

Dissolve 1 lb. sugar in a pint of water in a saucepan.
Now pour into a deep bowl 1 quart of honey (or maple
syrup), a little less still cider, $1/2$ glass of kirsch and $1/2$
lb. melted fresh butter. Chop fine $1/2$ candied orange and
$1/2$ lemon peel and add, together with the grated rind of
1 lemon. Then add $1/2$ lb. sugar, a little powdered aniseed, a pinch of cinnamon and nutmeg. Mix ingredients
well, then add 6 lbs flour and a tablespoonful of baking-
powder. Work thoroughly, form into 7 rounds and lay
on well-floured baking tin. Bake in a hot oven and brush
with syrup while hot. This gives the required glaze.

Leckerli
Basle

4 lbs honey, at least two years old, 2 lbs castor sugar, 5 lbs white flour, $^1/_2$ lb. each candied orange and lemon peel, 2 lbs blanched almonds, chopped with the peel, the grated rind of 2 lemons, 3 ozs cinnamon, 20 ground cloves. Put the honey in a thick pot, preferably iron, and melt till it comes to the boil. Add a small glass of kirsch, then the sugar, and replace the pot on the flame; add the spices and almonds and stir well. Pour in flour gradually and stir until the mixture begins to come away from the sides of the pan, in about $^1/_4$ hour. Dredge a pastry board with flour and turn the mixture out on to it. If it is too thin to roll, add more flour, but only if absolutely necessary. Roll out $^1/_4$—$^1/_2$ in. thick and stamp out the leckerli with the mould (oblong, 2 × 3 ins). Lay them carefully side by side on a well-floured baking-tin. Bake the following day, heating oven first.

When baked, the leckerli are cut apart, then brushed with the following glaze and left to dry: beat 4 whites of egg to froth and mix with $^1/_2$ lb. fine sugar for an hour.

Schlatemer Rickli
Schaffhouse

30 eggs, 3 lbs sugar, salt, 2 pinches carbonate of soda, 1 gill kirsch, 2 lbs butter, 8—9 lbs flour (for private use, take $^1/_{10}$ of these quantities). First mix the eggs well with the sugar, add the salt, carbonate of soda and kirsch and work in the flour by spoonfuls. Leave to stand overnight.

55

On the following day, roll out $1/4$ in. thick, then cut into oblongs $3 \times 3^{1}/_{2}$ in. with the pastry-cutter. Leaving a 1 in. wide border round each oblong, make four incisions lengthwise, so that the inside is divided into three strips. The middle strip is left as it is, the two to right and left being pulled out a little and woven over the edges of the oblongs. They are then fried in hot fat and strewed with sugar.

These fritters are *de rigueur* at weddings, and it is not unusual for two or three times the quantity here given to be made, especially when there is another gathering on the day following the wedding, when as many as eighty to a hundred women may be invited to coffee.

Cream Caramels
Toggenburg, Appenzell

Put 1 pint of cream or milk on flame in a saucepan. As soon as it rises, stir in $1/2$ lb. sugar. Stir till light brown, then spread on a tin first warmed and buttered and dusted with flour. At the end of 10 minutes cut out the caramels with a sharp knife or mould.

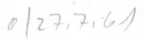